AGENT AR[...]
ON THE
STORMY
SEAS

Martin Oliver

Illustrated by Paddy Mounter
Designed by David Gillingwater

Cover design: Russell Punter and David Gillingwater

Series editor: Gaby Waters
Additional designs by Sarah Dixon

TED SMART

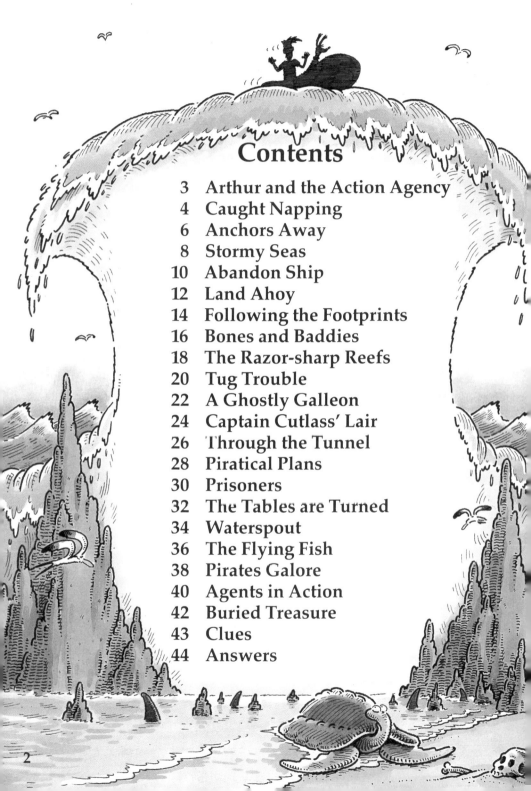

Contents

Arthur and the Action Agency

The Action Agency is a world wide undercover organization dedicated to fighting crime and solving mysteries. Supremely successful, the Agency lives up to its motto, *Search, Solve and Survive*, by operating a "go anywhere, do anything" service.

Arthur is the Agency's youngest recruit. His uncle is Jake Sharpe, the founder and brains of the Agency. He is an elusive figure and a master of disguise.

Uncle Jake has sent Arthur and his canine companion Sleuth, to Port Pacamac. Arthur checked his vital Agency information and kept his eyes peeled and ears open. A good Action Agent should always be on the alert.

You can join Arthur's adventure by solving the puzzles that appear on almost every page If you get stuck, you will find extra clues and all the answers at the back of the book.

Caught Napping

Arthur sat down in a crumbling quayside cafe. He ordered his favourite tutti-frutti cocktail and gazed out over Pacamac Bay. Despite what he had heard about ships disappearing, everything seemed normal.

"Uncle Jake must have thought we deserved a holiday," he said to Sleuth, who opened one eye then fell asleep again.

Arthur leant back and closed his eyes. He dreamt he was on a beach and all was quiet except for footsteps approaching then retreating into the distance.

Arthur woke up with a start, blinking in the sunlight. He looked down at the table. His drink had arrived – along with a grubby envelope. Sleuth snored quietly on while Arthur glanced around. There was no sign of the silent messenger.

Arthur ripped open the envelope. Inside he found a piece of paper covered with instantly recognizable symbols. It was a message from the Action Agency.

What does the message say?

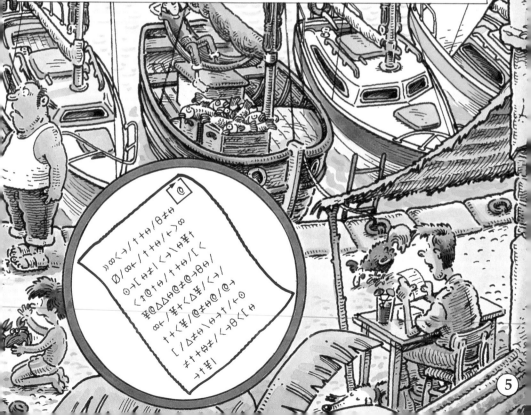

Anchors Away

Arthur spotted The Flounder, a three-masted schooner moored at the far side of the port. He dashed over to it. The captain smiled and took Arthur on as a deckhand. Introductions were hardly over before the captain boomed out orders to weigh anchor and cast off.

"We'll keep a low profile," whispered Arthur, as they set sail into the wide blue yonder. "And act like old sea-dogs."

But Arthur's stomach had different ideas. While Sleuth scampered round happily, Arthur struggled to find his sea-legs.

Arthur eventually got used to the motion of the ship, but there was hardly time to rest as the captain ordered "All hands on deck to learn ship safety."

"So much for a holiday," said Arthur, trying to concentrate on the ship's emergency drill.

For the first week The Flounder made good progress, sailing at full speed with a stiff breeze behind her.

Arthur learnt to steer as Captain Tar plotted their course through squalls, showers and schools of dolphins.

During the second week at sea, Kate spotted a dot on the horizon and shouted "Land Ahoy."

The crew anchored the boat and stepped onto a jetty. While Captain Tar traded some of their cargo, the others tried to get back their land-legs.

The following night Captain Tar gathered the crew together and told them a strange story.

"Ships disappear mysteriously in these waters," he said. "Some say the ghost ship of pirate Captain Cutlass still sails the seas, looking for victims."

On the third day's sail from the island, the wind died away. The sea became dead calm and the sails hung limply.

Arthur, Jim and Kate could only doze and dream as the air became hot and heavy. But Captain Tar didn't seem to mind.

They were still becalmed next morning when Arthur's night watch finished. Arthur was about to turn in when he saw Captain Tar tap the barometer uneasily.

"I hope those clouds don't mean trouble," yawned Arthur, as he headed below decks.

Stormy Seas

Arthur and Sleuth snoozed fitfully while the wind howled and waves broke against the porthole.

The Flounder sailed on as flashes of lightning streaked down from the dark clouds onto the sea.

Suddenly the ship listed over to port. Arthur and Sleuth flew out of their bunk and hit the deck.

Arthur picked himself up and desperately scrambled into his waterproofs. He and Jim dashed out of the cabin.

Up on deck, Kate and the captain were struggling with the wheel, trying to turn the ship to face the next wave.

But it was too late. An enormous wave raced towards The Flounder.

It towered high above the ship for a second, then broke over the prow.

Tons of salty water streamed across the deck, slamming into the crew.

Abandon ship.

The Flounder rolled and dipped under the weight of water, then slowly rose.

The main mast had snapped like a twig and the sails were in tatters.

Captain Tar roared orders above the gale, as the crew clung on for dear life.

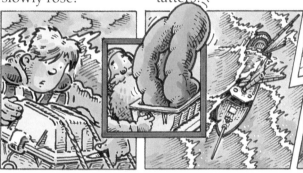

Jim cut through the lashings holding the life raft. Captain Tar pulled a ripcord to inflate it.

More waves crashed broadside into the stricken ship as Kate and Arthur scrambled below deck.

Water was pouring into the cabin as Kate grabbed vital equipment. Arthur tried the radio.

It was dead. Arthur yanked open a drawer in the captain's desk and grabbed the logbook, a map and a note. Arthur noticed something strange.

The note was in code. But he only had time to glance at it, before stuffing it into a pocket.

What does it say?

Abandon Ship

Arthur struggled out of the cabin and joined the others up on deck. He clung onto the guardrail as the ship rolled and pitched unsteadily. The life raft was already floating on the churning sea.

Kate got ready to join Jim aboard the raft. Clutching her equipment bag tightly, she leapt over the side.

Arthur gulped, it was his turn now. He picked up Sleuth and looked over. The raft bounced up and down in the heavy swell, banging against The Flounder's hull then drifting away.

"It's all in the timing," thought Arthur, just as a gust of wind blew him off the ship . . . and into the inflatable.

Kate untangled herself from the others and stared at The Flounder. Something was wrong.

"The mooring rope's snapped," she gasped.

As they helplessly watched the captain drift away, Jim realized the raft was taking in water. They had to bail it out, and fast.

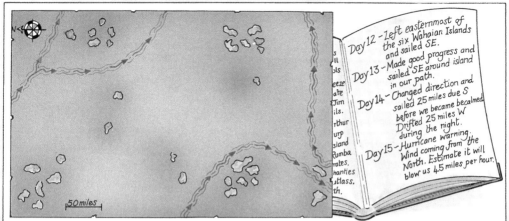

Five hours later the hurricane had blown itself out and the raft was floating in calm sea. Arthur opened the door flap and stared around. There was water, water everywhere, but no sign of The Flounder or of Captain Tar.

Sleuth growled at a shark and Arthur's mind raced back to his Shipwreck Survival Course.

They must try to pinpoint their position to see if they were near land. Jim checked the compass while Arthur studied The Flounder's logbook. Kate noticed they were drifting in a current. Arthur thought hard and picked up the chart. Now he could work out where they were.

Where are they?

Land Ahoy

During the damp and cramped night, Arthur decided to tell the twins about the Action Agency and to enlist their help on his mission. They listened in amazement and eagerly agreed to become Apprentice Action Agents. As dawn broke Arthur spotted low clouds on the horizon.

Just then a seabird landed by the raft. Sleuth licked his lips hopefully, while Arthur's brain whirred and clicked. Could these signs mean land ahead? Jim and Kate whooped happily at the thought and began paddling.

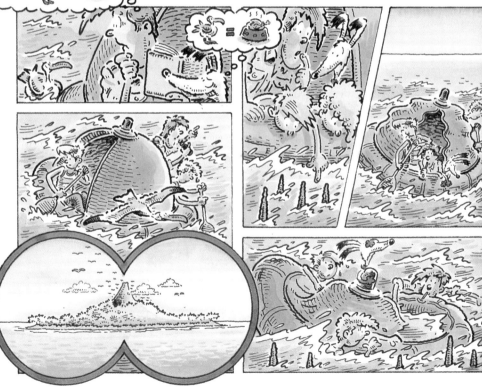

Arthur picked up his all-weather, extra-tough, mega-magnifying Action Agency issue binoculars and scanned the horizon. A coral island zoomed into focus.

"Land ahoy," he shouted.

Kate and Jim went into overpaddle. The raft raced along until Kate heard a rip, then a hissing sound. They were punctured! Arthur blew into the flotation chamber while the others tried to steer towards the island, avoiding more coral.

But it was no good. Despite all their efforts, they were still deflating fast.

"Abandon ship," panted Arthur.

They floated out of the raft and half-swimming, half-wading, dragged themselves ashore.

"Safe at last," gasped Jim, collapsing on the beach. "We're alone on a deserted island."

"Maybe we're not," said Kate.

What has Kate spotted?

Following the Footprints

Hmm, size 12 man's.

Arthur bent over to examine the footprints while Sleuth growled suspiciously at them. They were human, but were they friendly? The footprints led up the beach and disappeared into the dense undergrowth.

"Let's follow them," said Jim. "They may lead to civilization."

"Sleuth can sniff the way," Arthur replied. "We'll follow, but stay alert."

A parrot screeched overhead as the trio tramped uphill behind Sleuth, their mouths watering at the delicious-looking tropical fruits all around.

A few minutes later Sleuth barked angrily. The trail ended abruptly at a pool of water and a waterfall. Kate rested her sore feet while Jim wondered what they should do next.

Arthur looked up. Whoever had made the trail of footprints must have swum across the pool and climbed the cliff opposite.

After telling the twins to carry on searching, Arthur waded through the shallow water at the edge of the pool and began scrambling up the rocks. Trying not to look down, he gradually left Jim and Kate far behind.

It was a long hot climb, but at last Arthur reached the top. Once he had got his breath back, he wiped the sweat from his eyes and scanned the island hoping to see some trace of civilization or even of Captain Tar.

But there was no sign of human life, only a seabird that flapped its wings and gazed curiously back at him. Arthur slumped down dejectedly beside Sleuth. He wondered what they should do next. They didn't want to be stuck on a desert island.

Back at the pool Kate explored the waterfall but found nothing. She was swimming back, when Jim spotted a scrap of paper. He picked it up and realized it was written in code.

"I think it describes a trail," he shouted. "If we follow it we might find help."

"Or pirate treasure," Kate added hopefully. "But where can we pick it up?"

Where can they join the trail?

15

Bones and Baddies

Arthur paced around the cliff-top, flicking through his Agency Handbook for the chapter on shipwrecked sailors. He was concentrating so hard that he didn't hear Sleuth's warning bark until it was too late.

Arthur found himself falling through the air. He tried to stop his fall by grabbing hold of an overhanging vine, but it snapped off in his hand.

Arthur plummeted towards the ground, hoping for a soft landing. He looked down at the jungle below and crashed head first through the roof of an old hut, half-hidden amongst the thick trees and bushes.

Arthur slowly opened his eyes. He looked up and wished that he hadn't. His hair stood on end, then everything went black.

Meanwhile Kate and Jim were following the trail. Jim spotted two people ahead. He was about to rush up to them when Kate stopped him.

"I don't like the sound of what they're saying," she whispered. "Let's stay hidden."

Jim nodded and stepped back . . . onto a dry twig. It cracked loudly. Kate and Jim froze in horror then turned to run.

But it was too late. Before they could escape, they felt hands on their shoulders and unfriendly faces stared at them.

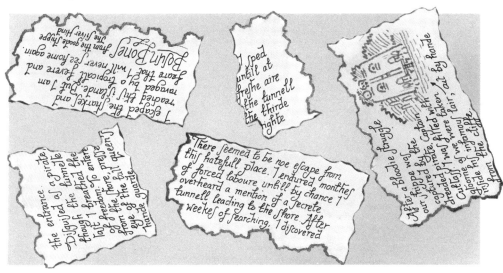

At that moment Sleuth licked Arthur back to consciousness. Arthur was about to race out of the hut when the remains of an old document caught his eye. He began fitting the bits together and working out the writing.

"What a find," thought Arthur, carefully tucking the pieces into his bulging bag. "I must show this to Jim and Kate."

What does the document say?

17

The Razor-sharp Reefs

A rthur was heading back towards the waterfall when Sleuth sniffed the air and growled. Arthur glimpsed movement on the beach. He looked closer and gasped. Jim and Kate were being pushed into a rowing boat.

Arthur raced down through the trees and thick bushes to the beach. He stared across the lagoon. The twins were being taken towards a rusty old tug boat. Sleuth sniffed at a scrap of blue paper and gave it to Arthur.

"This is no time to pick up litter," hissed Arthur, putting it in his pocket. "We must find a way through the razor-sharp coral to that tug."

Can Arthur find a safe route to the boat?

Tug Trouble

A rthur trod water and oil as he tried to fathom out a way aboard the old tug. He heaved himself out of the water to reach a porthole in the side of the ship. But he couldn't make it.

Then Arthur had a flash of inspiration and swam over to the slimy anchor chain. He hoisted himself up link by slippery link, until at last he clambered over the side of the ship.

He landed on the deck and hid behind a battered funnel. He peered out and saw the twins being led below decks by two mean-looking villains. Who were these crooks? Why had they kidnapped Jim and Kate?

Arthur turned to Sleuth, but he wasn't there. Arthur looked back over the side and spotted a dorsal fin. He threw Sleuth a line and hauled him up, just in time. Sleuth collapsed in a damp puddle and the tug set sail.

Hours later the boat was echoing to the sound of snoring as the stowaways crept out from behind the funnel. Arthur stared inside the wheelhouse, trying to find Jim and Kate. Then he tiptoed below decks to check out the crew's quarters.

Arthur followed his nose and peered in at the galley. He left quickly. Sleuth led the way down to another deck and growled outside a steel door. Kate and Jim were in the cabin ahead. They seemed to be all right but they were well guarded.

Just then Arthur heard footsteps coming their way. He stared round in horror then dived through an open door into the engine room. Arthur hid behind the steamy old engine and strained to hear the muffled conversation outside.

His heart sank as he heard the key click in the lock. He was trapped! Arthur looked round the grimy room and spurred himself into action. There must be a way out, and he was going to find it.

Is there a way out?

21

A Ghostly Galleon

It was dark when Arthur managed to open the door and he crept silently above decks. The ship was moored in a lagoon. The moon was shining and mist rose off the sea. In the distance Arthur spotted Jim and Kate being rowed towards an island.

Just then Sleuth's hackles rose as a faint chugging noise drifted over the water. Suddenly an old sailing ship appeared through the mist. Arthur stared wide-eyed at the tattered sails, the skull and cross bones and the ghostly crew.

"H .. h .. help," he quavered, his hair standing on end.

Arthur remembered Captain Tar's story and turned white. His Agency Training hadn't covered spooky spectres, and this looked very much like the ghostly galleon of pirate Captain Cutlass.

Is it?

Captain Cutlass' Lair

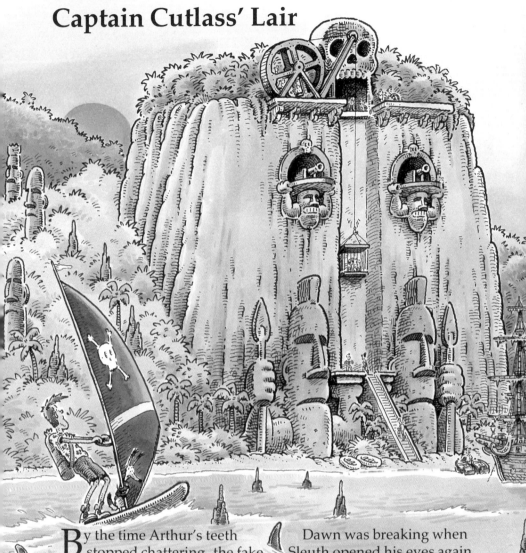

By the time Arthur's teeth stopped chattering, the fake ghosts had changed course for the island that the twins had been taken to. Were the kidnappers in league with the creepy crew? There was only one possible way to find out.

"We'll follow them," Arthur said, lowering a sail board into the water. "Hang on Sleuth."

Dawn was breaking when Sleuth opened his eyes again. Arthur windsurfed unsteadily round a headland and gasped.

He spotted the twins. They were inside a cage being winched up a fortress-like cliff. Arthur stared in amazement and thought back to the memoirs of Bosun Bones. This was the entrance to Captain Cutlass' pirate lair.

Arthur swung the sail round, regained his balance and headed for dry land. At last he beached the board out of sight of the villains. Sleuth bounded happily onto solid ground and scampered round the huge stone heads that were scattered along the shore.

"I must try to rescue Jim and Kate and find out what these crooks are up to," Arthur thought. "But the front entrance is impregnable. If only there's a back way in."

Arthur began scrambling up the steep hill for a better view of the base. Suddenly he tripped over the overgrown head of a fallen statue.

As he picked himself up, his memory jolted into gear and he reached for Bosun Bones' memoirs. Maybe there was a way into the base after all?

How can Arthur get in?

Through the Tunnel

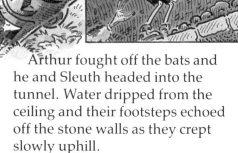

Arthur climbed the head and pressed the eye. There was a grinding sound below and a stone slab slid open. Arthur shone his torch into the blackness and the air was full of dark flying shapes.

Arthur fought off the bats and he and Sleuth headed into the tunnel. Water dripped from the ceiling and their footsteps echoed off the stone walls as they crept slowly uphill.

Sleuth was first out of the tunnel and into the cave. He sniffed the air then listened out by the door. Arthur picked up some photos on a desk. He stared hard at them. His brain whirred as he spotted the two kidnappers, the fake ghost ship and its crew.

Arthur immediately recognized the names of the boats in the photos. That solved the mystery of the missing ships. Arthur smiled grimly. The first part of his mission was complete; now to find out more about these modern-day pirates.

Suddenly Arthur stopped. Ahead he spotted light at the end of the tunnel. Arthur and Sleuth cautiously scrambled over fallen stones, peered through the hole and gasped.

The cave in front of them was crammed full of radar screens and hi-tech tracking equipment. But there was no trace of Kate and Jim or any other sign of life. What was going on?

to organization spider and mangler
max lil patch eye the have we the
for route ship target next fish
flying the sail will it the between
sw and graveyard ships island
peaks twin the reaching until the
of northernmost here needles three
turn will it nw head and with level
until in island easternmost then
archipelago diamond cruise will it
between s due and island shark then
and volcano our of out an if
territory use occurs emergency jpx
plan escape

Who was behind the villains, and what was their next target? Just then a printer chattered into life. Arthur hardly had time to memorize the coded type before Sleuth growled. Seconds later the door opened and a familiar figure walked in.

Arthur peered at the pirate. If she was here, the twins must be nearby. But before Arthur started searching for them, he tried to decode the message. It might answer some questions.

What does the message say?

Piratical Plans

The pirates were being masterminded by the Spider Organization, the most powerful group of criminals in the world and sworn enemies of the Action Agency. Arthur's brain grappled with this incredible information as he crept away and found himself in a huge cave.

He peered down and gasped. He had found the nerve centre of the operation. A 3-D map dominated the room while machines bleeped and whirred. To his right Arthur spotted the twins. Max Mangler snarled at them and gave orders to a burly henchman.

Suddenly Eye Patch Lil rushed into the cave shouting orders. Arthur thought back to the coded message. If he could work out where The Flying Fish was going to be attacked, he might be able to foil the piratical plan.

Arthur studied the map. As he did so he heard a hissing noise behind him. His head began to swim as he slumped to the floor.

Where will The Flying Fish be attacked?

Prisoners

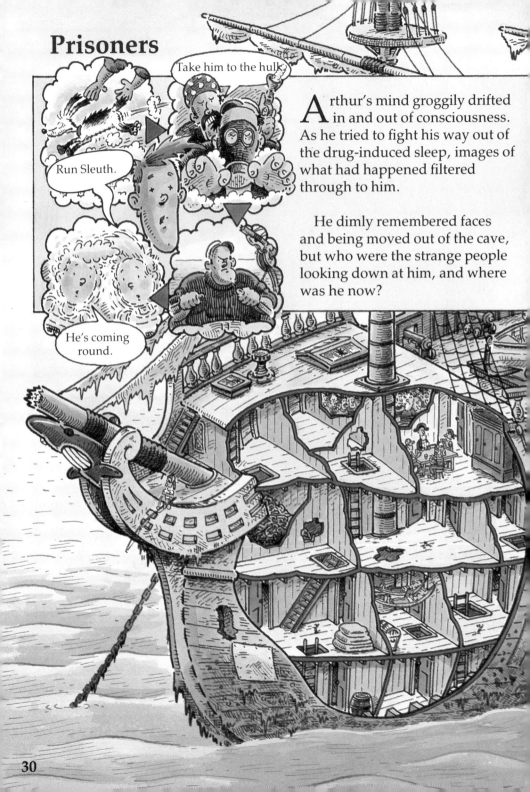

Arthur's mind groggily drifted in and out of consciousness. As he tried to fight his way out of the drug-induced sleep, images of what had happened filtered through to him.

He dimly remembered faces and being moved out of the cave, but who were the strange people looking down at him, and where was he now?

We're aboard the prison ship and we can't move unless we untie these ropes.

Arthur blinked again at the two blurs staring at him. Kate and Jim suddenly appeared.

They explained the situation and Arthur's mind snapped back into action. He heard a strange noise coming from the porthole.

"Good work," whispered Arthur, as a bedraggled Sleuth squeezed into the cabin. "Bite through our ropes and we'll try and find a way up on deck. From there we might be able to escape."

How can they get up on deck?

The Tables are Turned

Arthur was first up on deck. He hid behind the capstan as the twins scrambled out of the hatch behind him.

"We must keep quiet until the coast is clear," whispered Arthur. "Once the pirates have gone below we will try to take a boat and reach The Flying Fish before it's attacked."

They heard laughter from the deck below and peered round the mast. Kate clenched her fists at what she saw.

"Those are the crews of the captured ships," she said. "We can't leave them as prisoners."

Kate was right, but there were only three of them against the pirates. Arthur gritted his teeth. He was an Action Agent. There was only one thing to do.

"Charge," yelled Arthur, grabbing a rope and swinging into a crowd of pirates. The twins followed up with a barrel.

The pirates were so surprised that they hardly had time to react before the captured crews joined in on Arthur's side. They soon turned the tables on the dastardly pirate crew.

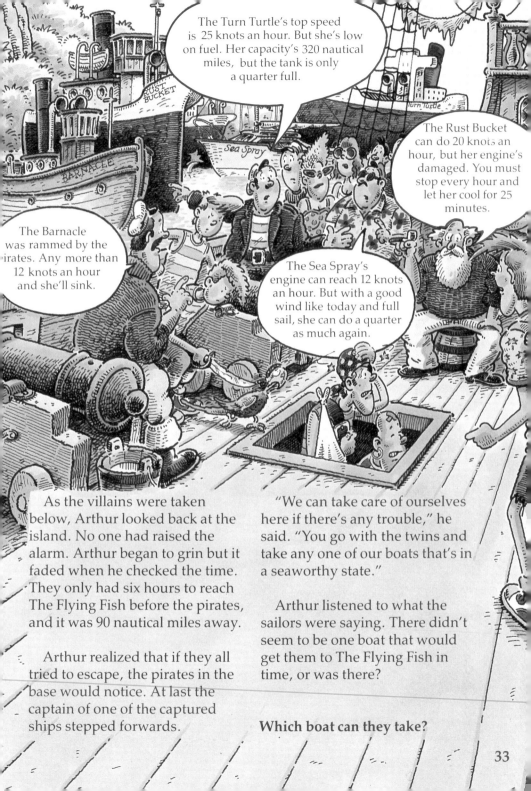

As the villains were taken below, Arthur looked back at the island. No one had raised the alarm. Arthur began to grin but it faded when he checked the time. They only had six hours to reach The Flying Fish before the pirates, and it was 90 nautical miles away.

Arthur realized that if they all tried to escape, the pirates in the base would notice. At last the captain of one of the captured ships stepped forwards.

"We can take care of ourselves here if there's any trouble," he said. "You go with the twins and take any one of our boats that's in a seaworthy state."

Arthur listened to what the sailors were saying. There didn't seem to be one boat that would get them to The Flying Fish in time, or was there?

Which boat can they take?

Waterspout

Jim and Kate helped Arthur aboard The Sea Spray. Kate went below to start the engine and the motley crew sprang into action. Arthur pulled out his Agency compass and grabbed the rudder. Jim pumped out the bilges, while Sleuth tried to hoist the sails.

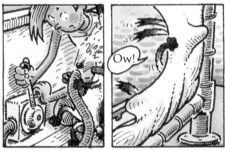

Wishing that Captain Tar was there to help, Arthur steered a course through the choppy water. Kate left the engine and acted as lookout. They made good headway despite heavy seas.

After five hours rolling and pitching, Kate spotted something on the horizon.

"Look out," she yelled. "It's a waterspout."

Arthur's blood froze as the column of water raced towards them. There was no escape. Gale force winds blasted around them and they were sucked into the whirling waterspout.

Arthur felt himself being lifted up, spun round and round, then hurled deep into the water. His head was spinning and his lungs were bursting as he swam up to the surface. At last his head broke through the water and he gulped down fresh air. Still gasping for breath, he tried to think. Even his Action Agency Training hadn't covered this situation.

Arthur spotted Sleuth floating amongst the remains of the boat. As Sleuth clung onto Arthur's equipment bag, Jim and Kate swam over towards them. Arthur saw a large piece of wreckage floating nearby and spluttered out orders to the others.

"We're in a bad way," Arthur muttered, clambering onto the makeshift raft. "No food, no water, no sign of help."

Just then Kate shouted "Ship ahoy!" and pointed to a dot on the horizon. The crew jumped up and down waving. But it was no good. The ship kept going.

Arthur emptied out his bag and thought back to Captain Tar's emergency signals. If only he could remember the correct signals and find something to signal with.

What can they use to signal? What signals should they use?

Get aboard the wreckage. We'll use it as a raft.

The Flying Fish

We've escaped from some ruthless pirates.

As the gleaming boat lowered rescue nets and powered towards the raft, Kate pointed to the name painted on its bows. Arthur gasped. It was The Flying Fish. They began climbing up and Arthur glanced at his watch, there was no time to lose.

At last Arthur pulled himself up and over the guard rail. As soon as his feet touched the deck, he looked round for the captain then raced towards him. The captain backed away, looking worried as Arthur began telling him about the pirates.

Wow!

This is our cargo.

The captain listened kindly, then led Arthur and the twins out of the sun. He took them below decks, past cameras and thick steel doors.

Why was there so much security? Kate asked the captain who unlocked a door and showed them into a room . . .

It was packed full of gold, jewels and treasure. Arthur and the twins gasped.

"These art treasures belong to world-famous museums. We are shipping them to . . ." the captain began when he was suddenly interrupted by a shout from above: "Raft ahoy."

The Action Agents were hard on the heels of the captain as he raced up to the bridge, picked up his telescope and trained it on a floating speck.

"More shipwreck victims," the captain muttered. "Probably hit by the waterspout. Stop engines. Stand by to pick them up."

Arthur peered through the telescope and stared closely at the shipwrecked sailors on the raft. Suddenly he noticed that some things were very wrong.

"Don't stop," he yelled frantically. "It's a trap."

What has Arthur noticed?

Pirates Galore

In the nick of time, the captain ordered "Full steam ahead" and swerved his ship past the fake survivors.

"Hooray," shouted Kate, but she was cut short by Sleuth's warning bark.

The sea frothed and churned as a submarine surfaced beside the furious pirates. They abandoned their swamped raft and scrambled aboard the menacing craft.

"Torpedo," screamed Jim. "Coming straight for us."

As they raced for the islands Arthur ran into the bridge and frantically tried to radio for help. But it was no good, his messages were being jammed. Then Sleuth growled angrily. Arthur looked up and gasped in horror.

The pirate ship was right beside them. Arthur spotted Eye Patch Lil snarling as she prepared to fire the cannons.

"All hands on deck," yelled Kate. "Stand by to repel boarders."

Torpedoes to port and starboard.

The captain flicked the engine to full throttle, but the torpedo was still on a collision course. Jim braced himself for the inevitable explosion just as the ship accelerated and lifted itself out of the water. The torpedo passed harmlessly underneath.

Jim opened his eyes in amazement. They were aboard a hydrofoil. The captain took evasive action and set a course for the shallow water and safety of the Roba Roba islands. Kate shouted warnings as they zigzagged to avoid torpedoes.

Arthur reached the prow. He saw the Roba Roba Islands ahead and more ships speeding in from starboard. They were trapped! Arthur recognized a figure on one of the boats. It was Captain Tar – so he was a pirate too!

Arthur thought back to the message he had found aboard The Flounder. Then he remembered Agency Memo 522. Maybe it would be all right after all.

Are they trapped?

Agents in Action

Hello shipmates.

As the marine detachment of Action Agents sped towards the pirates, Captain Tar leapt aboard The Flying Fish grinning happily and shouting helloes.

"Captain Tar, how did you..?" began Jim, but he broke off as the boat swung round and headed for the pirates, who had turned tail and scattered over the sea.

The villains tried to sail for safety, but they were no match for the Action Agents. The Flying Fish sped over the waves and rammed the pirates' flagship. Action Agents began to round up waterlogged villains.

Arthur studied each of the captured pirates but there was no sign of Max or Lil. Just then Sleuth growled a warning. Arthur spotted some boats escaping in different directions.

"Max and Lil must be in one of those boats," shouted Kate.

The other agents had their hands full. It was up to Arthur to give chase. He stared at the boats and remembered decoding something about an escape plan.

"Follow me," Arthur yelled, jumping on a handy jetski. "I know which boat they are in."

Which is Max and Lil's boat?

Buried Treasure

Arthur followed the escaping villains. Up ahead he spotted a familiar-looking island and gasped. This was where he and the twins were first marooned.

Arthur jumped off his jetski. He sprinted up the beach then stopped in amazement. Max and Lil were swinging in a large net. Who had caught them?

Just then a tall figure strode out of the jungle. Sleuth wagged his tail happily.

"Uncle Jake!" gasped Arthur.

"Congratulations," he boomed, "Operation Skull and Crossbones has been a great success. Now we must find where these pirates buried their ill-gotten gains."

The captured villains shouted out defiantly. Sleuth barked and tugged at Arthur's pocket. Arthur pulled out a scrap of blue paper. The twins recognized it as Arthur decoded it.

"We know where the loot is," they all yelled. "Come on."

Where is the treasure buried?

You may have caught us, but you'll never find our loot. The Spider Organization can get hold of it whenever they want.

Clues

You will need to hold this page in front of a mirror to read the clues.

Pages 4-5

Look at the Action Code on page 3.
A = ⇒ B = ⇒

Pages 8-9

This is not simple until you get the hang of it. First think backwards, then try swapping the last letter of the first word with the last letter of the next word.

Pages 10-11

Follow the directions in the logbook on the chart.

Pages 12-13

Look carefully at the footprints on the beach.

Pages 14-15

First decode the message on the piece of paper, then use your eyes.

Pages 16-17

Trace over the document fragments then piece them together.

Pages 18-19

Arthur must not touch the coral, but he can scramble over rocks.

Pages 20-21

The key is in the lock on the other side of the door. Is there any way Arthur can reach it?

Pages 22-23

You don't need a clue for this. Just keep your eyes peeled.

Pages 24-25

Read through Bosun Bones' memoirs again.

Pages 26-27

Swap the first word with the third word then swap the fourth word with the sixth word and so on until the end of the message.

Pages 28-29

Plot the course of The Flying Fish and the attack course. Where do they both meet?

Pages 30-31

Avoid any cabins with pirates in them.

Pages 32-33

Look at what the sailors are saying. One nautical mile an hour is one knot.

Pages 34-35

Can they use anything to reflect the sun? Look back to the emergency drill on page 6.

Pages 36-37

This is easy. Use your eyes.

Pages 38-39

Decipher the Agency Memo on page 3 and check the message on page 9.

Pages 40-41

Flick back to the message on page 27. Does it mention an escape plan?

Page 42

Look back at the piece of paper on page 15. What is the final instruction?

Answers

Pages 4-5

The message is written in Action Code. This is what it says:

JOIN THE CREW OF THE FLOUNDER. INVESTIGATE THE DISAPPEARANCE OF SHIPS IN THIS AREA AND PREVENT FURTHER INCIDENTS.

Pages 8-9

The note has been written backwards and the first letter of each word has been swapped with the first letter of the next word. This is what it says with punctuation added:

EMERGENCY: HURRICANE IMMINENT – ALL CAPTAINS INVOLVED WITH OPERATION SKULL AND CROSSBONES ARE ORDERED TO RUN FOR COVER. REGROUP AT ROBA ROBA ISLANDS FLYING CORRECT IDENTIFICATION FLAG.

Pages 10-11

Arthur and the twins are here.

Arthur first works out where they were before the hurricane struck. He does this by plotting their course from the information in the captain's logbook. The course is marked in black. This tells Arthur where they were before the hurricane struck.

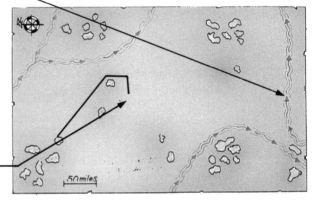

The last entry in the logbook tells Arthur that they have been pushed by a north wind at 45 miles an hour. Arthur knows that the hurricane lasted five hours. He works out that they are 225 miles south of their position when the hurricane struck.

This position also ties up with the information the twins have given Arthur, that they are in strong current heading East.

Pages 12-13

Kate has spotted a trail of footprints that does not match any of their footprints.

This trail has been made by someone who is barefoot.

44

Pages 14-15

Kate and Jim first decode the trail directions on the scrap of paper. They are written backwards with the letter "i" inserted after every three letters. This is what they say:

Jim and Kate then look around and spot a rock with a skull shape carved into it. This must be skull rock where they can pick up the trail.

FROM BUCCANEER BEACH HEAD FOR SKULL ROCK THEN GO EAST THROUGH THE JUNGLE TO GOLDEN BEACH. BURY LOOT SIX FEET UNDER THE EAGLE ROCK.

Pages 16-17

Here is the document after it has been pieced together.

After a bloodie ſtruggle our ſhippe waſ captured by the dreaded pirate, Captain Cutlaſſ. I waſ filled with gloome aſ we were taken inſide hiſ infamouſ lair, cut by hande from the cliffe.

There ſeemed to be noe eſcape from thiſ hatefull place. I endured montheſ of forced laboure untill by chance I overheard a mention of a ſecrete tunnell leading to the ſhore. After weekeſ of ſearching, I diſcovered

the entrance. Diſguiſed aſ a pirate I ſped though the tunnelle untill at laſt I breathed the freſhe aire of freedom. To entere the tunnell from the ſhore, preſſe the thirde eye of the tall queen'ſ righte hande guarde.

I eſcaped the ſharkeſ and reached thiſ iſlande. But I am ravaged by a tropicall fevere and feare that I will never ſee home again.

Beſun Boneſ from the goode ſhippe The ſilver Hind

Pages 18-19

The safe route to the boat is marked in black. Although Arthur must not touch the razor-sharp coral, he can scramble over the grey rocks.

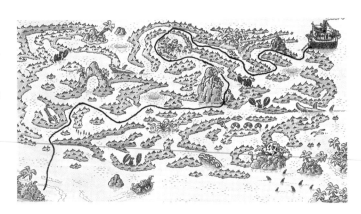

Pages 20-21

To escape, Arthur unfolds a newspaper and slides it through the large gap under the door. Next he pushes the key out of the lock with the screwdriver so that the key falls onto the newspaper Arthur then pulls the newspaper with the key on it back under the door towards him. Once he has the key, he can unlock the door from the inside.

Pages 22-23

Arthur spots several modern details that prove that the galleon is a fake ghost ship.

The giveaway details are ringed in black.

Pages 24-25

Arthur rereads Bosun Bones' memoirs. He realizes that he can get into the base via the secret tunnel that Bosun Bones found. To enter the tunnel, Arthur must press the third eye of the tall queen's right hand guard, here.

Pages 26-27

The message can be decoded by swapping the first word in the message with the third word, the fourth word with the sixth and so on until the end. This is what it says:

SPIDER ORGANIZATION TO MAX MANGLER AND EYE PATCH LIL. WE HAVE THE ROUTE FOR THE NEXT TARGET SHIP, THE FLYING FISH. IT WILL SAIL SW BETWEEN THE SHIP'S GRAVEYARD AND TWIN PEAKS ISLAND UNTIL REACHING THE NORTHERNMOST OF THE THREE NEEDLES. HERE IT WILL TURN AND HEAD NW UNTIL LEVEL WITH EASTERNMOST ISLAND IN THE DIAMOND ARCHIPELAGO. THEN IT WILL CRUISE DUE S BETWEEN SHARK ISLAND AND VOLCANO AND OUT OF OUR TERRITORY. IF AN EMERGENCY OCCURS USE ESCAPE PLAN JPX.

Pages 28-29

The Flying Fish will be attacked in this area.

Arthur works it out by plotting the course of The Flying Fish on the 3-D map. The route of The Flying Fish is marked in black.

Arthur then listens to the instructions that Eye Patch Lil shouts to the pirates. He realizes that The Killer Whale must be the name of the ship that will attack The Flying Fish. The attack course is given in the form of co-ordinates that match areas on the map. Arthur plots this course.

Where the two routes coincide is where The Flying Fish will be attacked.

Pages 30-31

The route up to the deck is marked in black.

Pages 32-33

Arthur knows that he has only six hours to reach The Flying Fish which is 90 nautical miles away. He did some sums based on what the sailors said.

The Turn Turtle only has enough fuel for 80 miles.

The Barnacle would take 7 hours to sail 90 miles.

The Rust Bucket would take 6 hours and 10 minutes to reach The Flying Fish.

The Sea Spray can do 15 knots at top speed. This would reach The Flying Fish in exactly six hours time.

The Sea Spray is the only boat Arthur can take.

Pages 34-35

Arthur can use the mirror or the lenses of the sunglasses to reflect the sun's rays and signal to the ship.

The signals he should use are the ones Captain Tar taught him aboard The Flounder on page 6.

Pages 36-37

Arthur recognizes these two men from the pirate base.

He also notices concealed weapons, a hidden radio and a periscope. They are all ringed in black.

These things convince Arthur that the men on the raft are pirates setting a trap.

Pages 38-39

Arthur realizes that Captain Tar is not a pirate and that they are therefore not trapped.

He works this out after first decoding Agency Memo 522. This says:

IN EMERGENCY ACTION AGENTS MAY TRANSMIT IN SIMPLE CODE. ALL SEABORNE AGENTS ACTIVE IN THIS AREA MUST CARRY BLACK AND RED IDENTIFICATION FLAG.

When Arthur sees Captain Tar and the ships speeding in from starboard, he spots that they are all flying black and red flags. This means that Captain Tar and the others must be Action Agents. Their location ties in with the instructions in the note Arthur found aboard The Flounder on page 9. Because the message was in simple code, not in Agency code, it must have been sent by an Action Agent.

Pages 40-41

Arthur decoded a message on page 27 which mentioned escape plan JPX. When Arthur looks at the getaway boats, he spots one boat with JPX written on it. This is Max and Lil's escape boat.

Page 42

Max and Lil buried their loot under the eagle rock.

This is the final direction on the coded trail written on the blue scrap of paper.

The twins dropped the note when they were captured on page 17. Sleuth gave it to Arthur on pages 18-19.

This edition produced for:
The Book People Ltd, Hall Wood Avenue, Haydock, St Helens WA11 9UL